Material Matters

Mixtures, Compounds & Solutions

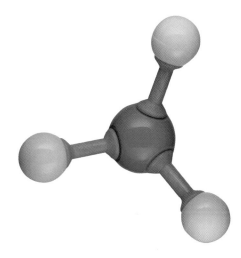

Carol Baldwin

Chicago, Illinois

For information, address the publisher:
Raintree, 100 N. LaSalle, Suite 1200, Chicago, IL 60602

Printed and bound in China
08 07 06 05 04
10 9 8 7 6 5 4 3 2 1

Library of Congress Cataloging-in-Publication Data
Baldwin, Carol.
  Mixtures, compounds, and solutions / Carol Baldwin.
    p. cm. -- (Material matters)
Includes bibliographical references and index.
Contents: Describing matter -- Building blocks of matter -- Elements -- Important compounds -- Mixtures -- Solutions-one type of mixture -- Other types of mixtures -- Alloys.
  ISBN 1-4109-0550-0 (lib. bdg.), 1-4109-0937-9 (Pbk.)
  1. Chemical elements--Juvenile literature. 2. Chemicals--Juvenile literature. [1. Chemical elements. 2. Chemicals. 3. Mixtures.] I. Title. II. Series: Baldwin, Carol, 1943-   Material matters.
  QD466.B23 2004
  540--dc22
                    2003011202

Acknowledgments
The publisher would like to thank the following for permission to use photographs:
P. 4 Maurice Nimmo/FLPA; pp. 4–5, 8, 14–15, 23 T. Waltham/Geophotos; pp. 5 (top), 16–17, 36, 36, 40, 45 Photodisc; p. 5 (middle), 26–27 Prof S. Cinti/CNRI/Science Photo Library; pp. 5 (bottom), 35 Foto Natura Catalague; p. 6 FLPA; pp. 6–7, 8–9, 10, 11, 12, 14, 22–23, 24, 34, 36–37, 38–39 Corbis; pp. 7, 20, 31, 41 Tudor Photography; p. 9 W. White/Corbis; pp. 10–11 Empics; pp. 12–13 CNRI/Science Photo Library; p. 15 Vanni Archive/Corbis; p. 16 Adam Hart Davis/Science Photo Library; p. 17 R. Brooks/FLPA; p. 18 J. L. Pelaez/Corbis; p. 19 M. Gerber/Corbis; p. 19 W. Meinderts/FLPA; pp. 20–21 D. Pebbles/Corbis; p. 21 Art Directors & Trip; p. 22 Robin Chittenden/FLPA; pp. 24–25 Bettmann/Corbis; p. 25 P. Souders/Corbis; p. 27 W. Wisniewski/FLPA; p. 28 Trevor Clifford; pp. 28–29 K. Fleming/Corbis; pp. 29, 44 G. Lepp/Corbis; p. 30 M. Walker/Art Directors & Trip; pp. 30–31 L. Lefkowitz/Corbis; pp. 32–33 Minden Pictures/FLPA; p. 33 O. Franken/Corbis; pp. 34–35 C. Cohen/Corbis; pp. 37–38 Science Photo Library; p. 39 Earth Satellite Corporation/Science Photo Library; pp. 40–41 S. Agliolo/Corbis; p. 42 Mark Thomas/Science Photo Library; pp. 42–43 H. Rogers/Art Directors & Trip; p. 43 L. Bergman/Corbis.
Cover photograph reproduced with permission of Topham Picturepoint.

Every effort has been made to contact copyright holders of any material reproduced in this book. Any omissions will be rectified in subsequent printings if notice is given to the publishers.
Disclaimer
All the Internet addresses (URLs) given in this book were valid at the time of going to press. However, due to the dynamic nature of the Internet, some addresses may have changed, or sites may have changed or ceased to exist since publication. While the author and publishers regret any inconvenience this may cause readers, no responsibility for any such changes can be accepted by either the author or the publishers.

Contents

Some words are shown in bold, **like this.** You can find out what they mean by looking in the glossary. You can also look out for them in the Word Bank at the bottom of each page.

Climbing High

Granite

In this piece of red granite, you can see the different particles that make up the rock. The particles are mixed together. Some parts of the rock have more dark particles than other parts do. Other parts have more light particles.

Each year, four million people visit Yosemite Valley in California. Every one of them sees the huge rock called Half Dome. But only a few people hike to the top. Half Dome rises 4,797 feet (1,462 meters) from the valley floor in Yosemite National Park, and it is a 14-mile (22.5-kilometer) hike to the top and back. Those who reach the top say the view is spectacular. But most do not even think about the rock they have climbed.

Half Dome is a huge dome of granite rock. All rocks are **mixtures** of **minerals** that naturally occur on the earth. Most granite is made of **particles** of the minerals quartz, mica, and feldspar. Minerals are chemical **compounds.**

Not all granite looks the same as the granite in Half Dome. Because granite is a mixture, granite from different places can be different colors.

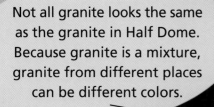

Word Bank   compound   substance made of atoms of more than one element
mixture   mix of elements or compounds not joined chemically

Compounds, mixtures, and solutions

Compounds form when substances come together and their particles join to form a new substance. Mixtures form when substances come together but their particles do not join. Most rocks used in buildings and monuments are mixtures of mineral compounds. Rocks and minerals are only a few of the compounds and mixtures around us. When we breathe air, we take in a mixture of gases. Most of the foods we eat are also mixtures. When we drink water, are we drinking a compound or a mixture? Well, it depends where the water comes from. Pure water is a compound. But most water has other substances mixed with it. That water is a special kind of mixture called a **solution.**

Turn to page 32 to find out what makes solutions special.

Find out later...

What compound is produced when the space shuttle lifts off?

What compound is found inside your stomach?

How can fish suffocate in water?

particles   tiny pieces
solution   mixture in which one substance dissolves in another

5

Describing Matter

Five kinds of matter

About 3,000 years ago, the Chinese thought that there were five kinds of matter. These were fire, wood, **metal,** earth, and water.

The Chinese thought that these forms could change from one to another. For example, wood can be burned. So wood could change to fire. When the fire goes out, ashes are left. Ashes were thought to be earth.

Everything around us is **matter.** Matter is anything that takes up space and has **mass.** The more mass something has, the heavier it is. The two types of matter are **pure substances** and **mixtures.** A pure substance has the same features throughout. Water and other **compounds** are pure substances. Mixtures do not have the same features throughout. Granite is a mixture that has more dark **particles** in some parts than in other parts.

Composition of matter

Compounds and mixtures are made of simpler pure substances called **elements.** Two or more elements join to form a new substance called a compound. Water is a compound of the elements hydrogen and oxygen. Two or more elements or compounds come together to make a mixture. But a mixture is not a new substance.

➤ ➤ ➤ ➤ ➤ ➤ ➤ ➤ ➤

Turn to pages 14 and 15 to read more about elements.

element   substance made of only one kind of atom
mass   amount of matter in an object. It is measured in grams or kilograms.

States of matter

Matter can take different forms. Most matter can be solid, liquid, or gas. These forms are called the **states of matter**.

A solid is a state of matter that stays the same shape no matter what container it is in. In a solid, particles of matter are tightly packed together. When matter is in its liquid state, it takes the shape of its container. A liquid like water also has particles that are close together. But the particles are not quite as close as they are in a solid and can move around each other more easily. Gas is a state of matter that also takes the shape of its container. But unlike a liquid, the particles of a gas spread out to take up all the space that is available.

An iceberg is water in its solid state, the ocean is water in its liquid state, and water vapor in air is water in its gas state. All three states of water are different forms of the same matter.

Half full or half empty?

Is a glass with some orange juice in it half full or half empty? Actually, neither, because it is completely full. The part of the glass that does not contain orange juice is filled with air. Air is a mixture of mostly nitrogen and oxygen gases. Even though they cannot be seen, these gases are matter. So they have mass and take up space.

Fast Fact

Water is unusual because its particles are farther apart in the solid (ice) than they are in the liquid state. This is why icebergs float in water and why water pipes can burst in winter. The water expands as it freezes.

There is more than just orange juice in this glass.

pure substance   matter that is the same throughout
state of matter   whether something is solid, liquid, or gas

Glow rocks

Some **minerals** have the unusual physical property of glowing when **ultraviolet (UV) light** is shined on them. Calcite rock is the compound calcium carbonate. Some samples of calcite glow red under UV light. Other mineral samples give off purple, green, or orange light.

Physical properties

A piece of copper wire will bend, but a piece of chalk will not. The chalk will break because it is **brittle**. Brittleness is a feature of chalk. Features like brittleness, color, size, and shape might change without changing what the chalk is made of. These features are **physical properties**. Smoothness and shininess are other examples of physical properties. Some physical properties describe how a material behaves. Being attracted by a magnet is a physical property of iron. **Elements** like copper and iron have physical properties that help identify them. So do **compounds** like chalk.

The different parts of a **mixture** also have physical properties. You can identify pebbles and sand in a mixture by the differences in their color, shape, and size.

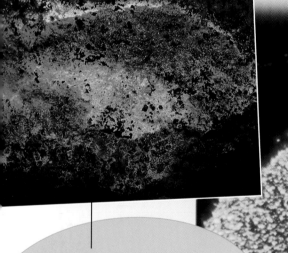

We cannot see UV light, but we can see some things that it shines on. This sample of uranium oxide glows green when UV light shines on it.

Word Bank   brittle   firm, but easily broken
physical change   change in how something looks, not in what makes it up

Physical changes

If you break a piece of chalk, you change its original size and shape. Some of its physical properties have changed. But the substance that makes up the chalk has not changed. A change in size or shape is a **physical change.**

A change in **state of matter** is also a physical change. If you heat a silver spoon to a high enough temperature, it will melt and change shape. But the silver is still silver. When water boils or freezes, it is still water. When it freezes and changes from a liquid to a solid, it is still water. These physical changes do not change what makes up water. Sawing wood, shredding paper, or mixing salt in water are also physical changes.

Diamonds have a very high melting point.

The temperature must reach 6,420 °F (3,550 °C) before a diamond will melt. That is two-thirds as hot as the surface of the sun. However, hydrogen melts at −434 °F (−259 °C) and boils at −423 °F (−253 °C). That is why hydrogen is a gas at room temperature.

One of the physical properties of rock is its state. When a volcano erupts, hot, liquid rock called lava pours out. When lava cools, it changes back to solid rock. This change of state is a physical change.

physical property feature that can be seen or measured without changing what a substance is made of

Chemical properties

A **chemical property** describes how a substance will react in the presence of another substance. For example, iron will react with oxygen in damp air to form rust. So reacting with oxygen is a chemical property of iron.

The ability of gasoline to burn in a racing car's engine is a chemical property of gas. The burning of fuel gives off **energy** needed to make the engine run. Other fuels, such as coal, natural gas, propane, and diesel are useful because they have the property of being able to burn.

Reacting with **acid** is also a chemical property. The **compound** bicarbonate of soda, or baking soda, will react with the acid in vinegar. So the ability to react with acid is a chemical property of baking soda.

Leaves change color due to a chemical change. A color change is one sign of a chemical reaction.

▶▶▶▶▶▶▶▶▶▶▶▶▶▶
Turn to page 26 to read more about acids.

The leaves on trees contain a chemical called chlorophyll that makes them green. In the fall, the chemical changes and the leaves lose their green color. In many trees, the red and yellow colors of other leaf chemicals can then be seen.

chemical property   feature of a substance that tells us how it will react

Chemical changes

A chemical change, or **chemical reaction,** happens when iron reacts with oxygen. A chemical reaction is a change in which one or more new substances are formed. The new substance formed during the reaction between iron and oxygen is the compound iron oxide, or rust. The rust formed is a new substance with new properties.

Burning wood is also a chemical change. Wood burns when it reacts with oxygen in the air. The new substances formed by this change are ash, carbon dioxide gas, and water vapor. Neither the powdery ash nor the two gases look or act like the wood.

Elements, compounds, and **mixtures** can all take part in chemical reactions.

Because the burning, or combustion, of gas takes place inside the engines of these cars, their engines are called internal combustion engines.

Hair colorists use chemical changes in their work. They use the compounds ammonia and hydrogen peroxide on a person's hair. This lets the hair **dye's** chemicals react with the hair's natural coloring chemicals. The reaction changes the person's hair color.

---

chemical reaction   change that produces one or more new substances

Building Blocks of Matter

More than 2,400 years ago, the Greek scientist Democritus said that it was not possible to keep dividing **matter** forever. At some point, the smallest piece would be reached that could not be divided further. He named this smallest piece an **atom.** The word atom comes from a Greek word that means "cannot be divided."

In the early 1800s, the English chemist John Dalton came up with a new idea about matter. The main parts of Dalton's atomic theory are:

- All **elements** are composed of atoms.
- Atoms cannot be divided or destroyed.
- Atoms of the same element are identical.
- Atoms of different elements are different.
- The atoms of two or more elements can join to form **compounds.**

Atomic power

We now know that it is possible to split atoms into even smaller **particles.** This can release huge amounts of **energy,** called nuclear energy. It can be seen when atoms are split in a nuclear power station or when an atomic bomb explodes.

▶ ▶ ▶ ▶ ▶ ▶ ▶
Turn to page 21 to learn more about ions.

Particles in atoms

All matter is made of atoms. Scientists have found that most of the **mass** of an atom is in its center. This center part of the atom is called the **nucleus**. The nucleus is made of two kinds of particle. **Protons** are particles with a tiny positive **electrical charge. Neutrons** are particles that are neutral, or have no charge.

Electrons are the third type of particle in atoms. They have a tiny negative electric charge. In an atom the number of electrons is the same as the number of protons. Their electric charges balance. So the atom is neutral. Sometimes, however, atoms can gain or lose one or more electrons. Then they become **ions**. Ions are either positively or negatively charged.

Where are the electrons?

Scientists used to think that electrons moved around the nucleus of an atom like planets move around the Sun. Today, scientists use a model called the electron cloud model. Exactly where the electrons are at any second is not known. They are moving very quickly somewhere in a cloud around the nucleus.

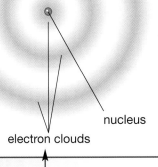

nucleus

electron clouds

Even if you magnify a human hair 1,000 times, you cannot see the individual atoms that make it up. It would take almost a million atoms lined up in a row to equal the thickness of a human hair.

Electrons are now thought of as clouds of negative charge around the nucleus of an atom.

Identifying elements

An **element** is made of only one kind of **atom.** All atoms of an element contain the same number of **protons** in their **nucleus.** For example, all oxygen atoms have eight protons in their nucleus. All aluminum atoms have thirteen protons. So scientists can classify elements by the number of protons in their atoms.

Metals

Elements are grouped into three different types. These are **metals, nonmetals,** and metalloids. Most elements, such as aluminum and iron, are metals. All metals except mercury are solids at room temperature. Mercury is a liquid. All metals share certain properties. They can be polished so that they look shiny. Heat and electricity move well through metals. Also, many metals can be stretched into thin wires, hammered, or shaped without breaking.

Metal ores

Metals are often found in nature in rocks called **ores.** Most ores are compounds of a metal and a nonmetal, such as oxygen or sulfur. Hematite is an ore compound of iron and oxygen. We mine hematite to get iron.

Sulfur is a yellow nonmetal element. It is often found deposited at the edges of geysers like this one in Yellowstone National Park.

▶ ▶ ▶ ▶ ▶ ▶ ▶ ▶ ▶ ▶ ▶ ▶

Turn to pages 42 and 43 to read about how we use **mixtures** of metals.

Word Bank   chemical symbol   short way of writing the name of an element
metal   element with certain properties

Nonmetals and metalloids

Most nonmetals are solids, such as sulfur and carbon, or gases, such as oxygen and nitrogen. Bromine is the only liquid nonmetal at room temperature. Nonmetals cannot be polished to make them look shiny. Heat and electricity do not move well through them. Also, nonmetals usually cannot be hammered, shaped, or pulled into wires.

A few elements have properties in between those of metals and nonmetals. These elements are called metalloids. All metalloids are solids. Electricity moves through them, but not as well as it does through metals. Silicon is a metalloid. It joins with oxygen to form the **compound** silicon dioxide, known as sand.

Chemical symbols are a short way of writing the names of elements. Symbols are either one or two letters. The first is always a capital letter. Some symbols are the first one or two letters of an element's name. Other elements have two-letter symbols that come from their Latin names.

Some symbols come from an element's name in another language. For example, the symbol for lead, Pb, comes from its Latin name, *plumbum*.

nonmetal   element without metallic properties
ore   metal found combined with other elements

15

Compounds

How many compounds?

More than 21 million compounds have been identified. Only about 90 elements combine in ways to form these compounds. The elements carbon, hydrogen, oxygen, and nitrogen form the largest number of compounds. Glucose is a compound of carbon, oxygen, and hydrogen.

Compounds are substances made of **atoms** of more than one **element** joined together. Water is a compound made of hydrogen and oxygen atoms. Table salt is a compound made of two elements, sodium and chlorine. In a compound the atoms of elements join in special ways that hold them tightly together.

Combining elements

In order for elements to join to make a compound, there must be a **chemical reaction.** For example, small pieces of iron called iron filings can be mixed with powdered sulfur. But the iron and sulfur do not join to form a compound. They just form a **mixture.** However, a chemical change will happen if the mixture is heated. Then a compound called iron sulfide forms.

Ammonia is a compound made by joining nitrogen and hydrogen. In this model of an ammonia **molecule,** white balls are hydrogen atoms and the blue ball is a nitrogen atom.

Properties of compounds

Compounds have properties different from the elements that make them up. Sugar is a compound of carbon, hydrogen, and oxygen. Carbon is a black solid. Hydrogen and oxygen are both colorless gases. The sugar that forms when they join is a white solid with a sweet taste.

Iron is a hard **metal** that is attracted by a magnet. Sulfur is a bright yellow **nonmetal.** The iron sulfide formed when they join together is not attracted by a magnet and is not yellow. When iron joins with oxygen gas, it forms iron oxide, or rust. Rust is a soft, crumbly solid, so it does not have the properties of either iron or oxygen.

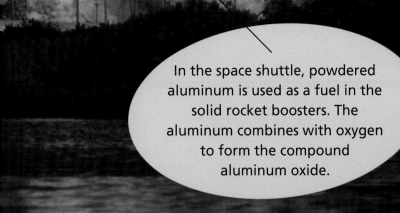

In the space shuttle, powdered aluminum is used as a fuel in the solid rocket boosters. The aluminum combines with oxygen to form the compound aluminum oxide.

Please pass the salt

Table salt is a compound of the elements sodium and chlorine. Sodium is a bright, silvery metal. It reacts violently with water. It is usually stored in oil to keep it from coming into contact and reacting with air or moisture. Chlorine is a poisonous, yellowish-green gas. But when the two elements combine, they form the salt that we sprinkle on food.

How carbon and oxygen join

Carbon dioxide usually forms when carbon burns in air. Each carbon atom joins with two oxygen atoms. But if carbon burns when there is not enough oxygen, it forms a compound called carbon monoxide. Each atom of carbon joins with just one atom of oxygen.

How elements join

Each different **compound** always contains the same **elements**. Also, the **atoms** in each compound always join in a certain way. Water always has two atoms of hydrogen for every atom of oxygen. That is why we write the **formula** for water as H_2O. Sometimes hydrogen and oxygen combine in a different way. Two atoms of hydrogen can join with two atoms of oxygen. This forms a different compound, called hydrogen peroxide. Hydrogen peroxide can be written as H_2O_2. Poured into glasses, the compounds look the same. But hydrogen peroxide has different properties from water. You can drink water, but you should not drink hydrogen peroxide. Hydrogen peroxide is used to kill **bacteria** on cuts and scrapes and to bleach hair.

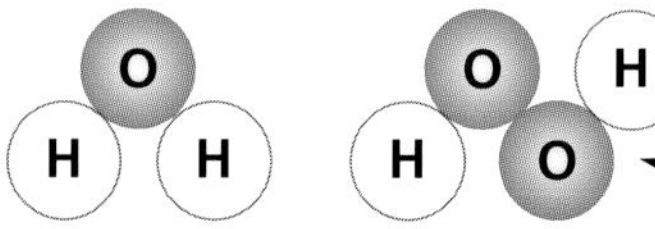

This diagram shows how atoms are arranged in **molecules** of water, H_2O, and hydrogen peroxide, H_2O_2.

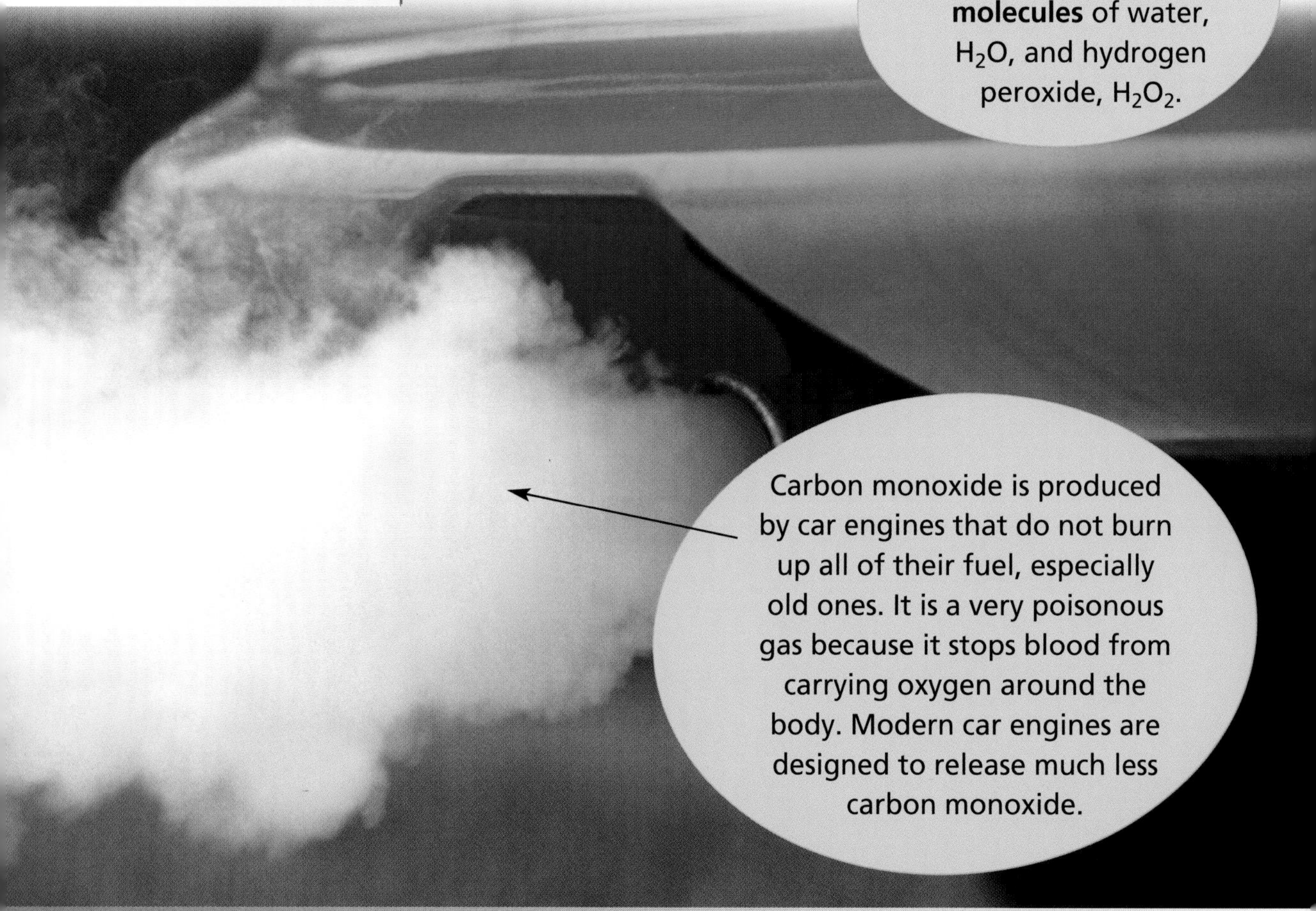

Carbon monoxide is produced by car engines that do not burn up all of their fuel, especially old ones. It is a very poisonous gas because it stops blood from carrying oxygen around the body. Modern car engines are designed to release much less carbon monoxide.

energy   ability to cause change
formula   symbols and numbers used to show how elements are joined

Breaking compounds apart

Chemical reactions are needed to break a compound apart. Often some kind of energy, such as heat, light, or electricity, is needed to make a reaction happen. Heating sugar will cause a chemical change that breaks the sugar apart. If sugar is heated long enough, only black carbon will be left in the container. The hydrogen and oxygen in the sugar join to form water vapor and go off into the air.

Light will make hydrogen peroxide break apart to form water and oxygen gas. That is why hydrogen peroxide is stored in dark bottles. Electricity can break apart salt, which is sodium chloride, to form sodium and chlorine.

Decomposers

Without decomposers, the earth would be covered with dead plants and animals and their waste.

Some living things, like molds and mushrooms, are called decomposers. That is because they break apart, or decompose, the compounds in dead plants, animals, and waste. The elements and simpler compounds go into the soil and can be used by new plants.

Hydrogen peroxide can make brown hair light blonde.

19

Hazardous materials

The type of bonding in a compound helps determine how **hazardous** the substance is. Many covalent compounds **evaporate** easily so they are easy to breathe in. Many are also flammable, or burn easily. This makes them dangerous compounds. They are often used in nail polish remover and some paint removers.

Molecules and covalent bonds

When two **atoms** join together, we say they form a **chemical bond.** A chemical bond usually involves a pair of **electrons**—one from each atom. However, not all chemical bonds are the same. **Compounds** are placed in two groups based on their chemical bonds.

A **covalent compound** contains atoms that share electrons in a bond. The smallest particle that shows the properties of a covalent compound is a **molecule.** Water is an important covalent compound. Each molecule of water contains two atoms of hydrogen and one atom of oxygen. The hydrogen and oxygen atoms share electrons to make the bonds in water molecules. Carbon dioxide is another covalent compound.

Uses: As a fuel for burners and as a household solvent. Harmful by inhalation, in contact with skin and if swallowed. Harmful: possible risk of irreversible effects through inhalation, in contact with skin and if swallowed. Keep locked up and out of the reach of children. Keep container tightly closed. Keep away from sources of ignition - No smoking. Wear suitable protective clothing and gloves. In case of accident or if you feel unwell seek medical advice immediately (show the label where possible). Contains Methanol.

HARMFUL

HIGHLY FLAMMABLE

Products containing compounds that evaporate or burn easily have warnings on their labels.

chemical bond   strong attraction between two atoms
covalent compound   compound formed when atoms join and share electro

Ions and ionic bonds

Table salt is not made of molecules. It forms when equal numbers of sodium and chlorine atoms join. Sodium is a **metal** and chlorine is a **nonmetal.** When a metal joins with a nonmetal, they form an **ionic compound.** Table salt is an ionic compound.

The metal and nonmetal atoms in an ionic compound do not share electrons. Instead the nonmetal atom takes one or more electrons from the metal atom. In table salt, each chlorine atom takes one electron from each sodium atom. When a sodium atom gives up an electron, it becomes positively charged. When a chlorine atom takes an electron, it becomes negatively charged. An atom, or a group of atoms, that has a positive or negative charge is called an **ion.** Ions with opposite charges group together.

Crystals

The shape of a crystal is determined by the way ions are arranged in it. Salt forms crystals that are cubes.

The force that holds ions together in an ionic bond is very strong. Many compounds that contain ionic bonds are solids that form **crystals.** An ionic crystal contains ions arranged in a regular pattern.

Both water and sand are examples of covalent compounds.

ionic compound   compound formed when a nonmetal takes electrons from a metal

Nitrogen oxides

Nitrogen combines with oxygen to form different oxides. Nitrogen oxide, NO, is a gas released from car exhausts. Nitrogen dioxide, NO_2, is a gas that forms when nitrogen oxide reacts with more oxygen. Dentists use dinitrogen oxide, N_2O, to relax patients. It is commonly called laughing gas.

Chemical formulas

Chemical symbols of **elements** are used to write **formulas**. A formula shows how many **atoms** of each element are joined together. The formula for oxygen in the air is O_2. The O stands for oxygen. The small 2 tells us that the atoms of oxygen are joined together in pairs.

Formulas are also used to write the names of **compounds**. If only one atom of an element is part of a compound, no number follows the symbol. For example, the formula for carbon monoxide is CO. That means there is one atom of carbon and one atom of oxygen in each **molecule** of carbon monoxide. The formula for carbon dioxide is CO_2. That means there is one atom of carbon and two atoms of oxygen in each molecule of the compound carbon dioxide.

Fast Fact

The chemical formula for table sugar is $C_{12}H_{22}O_{11}$. That means a molecule of sugar has 12 carbon atoms, 22 hydrogen atoms, and 11 oxygen atoms.

Nitrogen dioxide is an air **pollutant**. It causes the brownish smog sometimes seen over large cities.

compound ion   group of atoms that has an electric charge and acts together in a chemical reaction

Naming compounds

There are a few rules that can help you to name compounds containing a **metal**:

- Write the metal's name first.
- If the compound contains only one **nonmetal**, write the nonmetal's name second and change its ending to *ide*. For example, if a compound has sodium and chlorine in it, the second part of the name becomes *chloride*. So the compound's name is sodium chloride.
- If the compound contains oxygen and another nonmetal, the ending of the nonmetal's name becomes *ate*. For example, a compound of potassium, carbon, and oxygen is named potassium carbonate.
- If a compound does not contain a metal but is made of two nonmetals, the second nonmetal ends in *ide*. For example, compounds of carbon and oxygen are called carbon monoxide or carbon dioxide.

Compound ions

A **compound ion** is a group of covalently bonded atoms that has a positive or negative electrical charge. In **chemical reactions,** the group acts together as one charged ion. Some compound ions and their charges are shown in the table below.

Name	Formula	Charge
Ammonium	NH_4^+	+1
Hydroxide	OH^-	−1
Nitrate	NO_3^-	−1
Carbonate	CO_3^{-2}	−2
Sulfate	SO_4^{-2}	−2
Phosphate	PO_4^{-3}	−3

The words *mono-, di-* and *tri-* mean the numbers 1, 2, and 3. So carbon monoxide, a poisonous gas found in car exhaust fumes, has one carbon atom and one oxygen of atom. Carbon dioxide, making the bubbles in this soft drink, has two oxygen atoms.

This limestone is calcium carbonate. Its chemical formula is $CaCO_3$.

Important Compounds

Water in foods

Most foods contain some water.

Food	Percent water
Celery	94
Tomatoes	93
Spinach, raw	92
Strawberries	90
Oranges	86
Apples	85
Bananas	76
Eggs, uncooked	74
Macaroni, cooked	72
Chicken, grilled	71
Turkey, roasted	62
Beef, raw ground	54
Ham, cooked	54
Bread, whole wheat	35
Honey	15

Water is the most important **compound** on the earth. All living things contain water, so without water, life would not be possible.

Water cycle

Water on the earth is always moving and changing forms. The movement of water on the earth is called the **water cycle.** The Sun's **energy** makes some water change to water vapor. The water vapor rises into the air where it cools and forms clouds. Tiny droplets inside clouds join to form bigger drops. Finally, the drops fall as rain, snow, sleet, or hail. Rain or melted ice runs off the land into streams and rivers. This water flows into lakes and oceans and the whole cycle repeats.

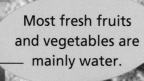

Most fresh fruits and vegetables are mainly water.

Word Bank   reduction   separating oxygen and metal from an ore

Ores

An **ore** is a compound from which a useful **metal** can be removed. Most ores are compounds made of a metal with one or more **nonmetals.** An ore of a metal joined with oxygen is called an oxide. Iron oxide, copper oxide, and aluminum oxide are ores. An ore of a metal joined with sulfur is called a sulfide. Lead sulfide and zinc sulfide are ores. A carbonate ore is a metal combined with carbon and oxygen. Magnesium carbonate is an ore.

We get useful metals from these compounds by using **chemical reactions** to break them apart. The metals are used to make cars, electrical wires, airplanes, bridges, and many other things.

Removing metal from ore

Useful metals are separated from oxide ores by a process called **reduction.** Oxides of many ores can be reduced using a form of carbon called coke.

In this blast furnace, coke reduces iron oxide to iron. Carbon dioxide gas is also produced.

These prehistoric cave paintings at Lascaux, France, were made with ochre. Ochre is an iron oxide that occurs naturally. It is formed by the reaction of oxygen in the air with rocks that contain iron.

Uses of sulfuric acid

Sulfuric acid is an important industrial compound. The pie chart below shows some of its uses.

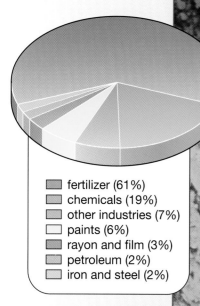

- fertilizer (61%)
- chemicals (19%)
- other industries (7%)
- paints (6%)
- rayon and film (3%)
- petroleum (2%)
- iron and steel (2%)

Acids

Acids are another group of important **compounds.** Acids are compounds that contain hydrogen and have a sour taste. Weak acids are found in many foods. Lemons, tomatoes, and vinegar all have acids in them. **Cells** in our bodies also contain a number of weak acids. These compounds help to keep us alive and healthy.

Strong acids can burn skin and are poisonous. Hydrochloric acid and sulfuric acid are strong acids. Hydrochloric acid is used to clean stone buildings and swimming pools. Sulfuric acid is used to make fertilizers, dyes, and fabrics such as rayon. In addition, sulfuric acid is used in car batteries andin paper manufacturing.

This microscopic picture shows the stomach lining. Hydrochloric acid is found in our stomachs. It helps break down foods we have eaten.

alkali   base that will dissolve in water

Bases

Bases are metal hydroxide or metal oxide compounds. They have a bitter taste and feel slippery. Bases are also called **alkalis** if they **dissolve** in water. Strong bases are poisonous and can cause serious burns. Lye, which is sodium hydroxide, is strong enough to dissolve animal bones. Drain cleaner and oven cleaner are strong bases that are used for cleaning.

Antacids are used to soothe upset stomachs. Antacids contain small amounts of a weak base, such as calcium hydroxide or aluminum hydroxide. These weak bases react with hydrochloric acid in the stomach. Bicarbonate of soda, or baking soda, is also a weak base that is used in cooking. Ammonia water is a weak base used in many household cleaning products.

Fast Fact
Wet soap is slippery because it contains a base.

Desert soils

Desert soils contain **minerals,** such as calcium carbonate, that are bases. Very little rain falls in deserts so these minerals do not get washed away. Plants like mesquite, aloe, Joshua trees, and cactuses are able to grow in desert soils.

base   compound that feels slippery and has a pH of more than than 7
cells   building blocks that make up all living things

Epsom salts

Epsom salts contain the compound magnesium sulfate. Epsom salts are used to help heal certain kinds of skin rash. They were named after Epsom, England, where they were discovered in well water. They have been used since the 17th century.

Salts

Salts are **compounds** that form when an **acid** reacts with a **base**. Sodium chloride, the best-known salt, has thousands of uses. Only a small amount of the sodium chloride produced by salt factories is put on the food we eat. All living things need some salt to live. Meat packers use salt to preserve meat. Salt is also used for making glass, treating leather, and making other chemicals.

Other salts are also important. Potassium nitrate is used in making fertilizers and explosives. Ammonium chloride is used in batteries. Silver bromide is used in making film for cameras. Sodium bicarbonate is used in baking powder and for making glass. Many other products around the home contain salts. They include baking soda, toothpaste, and deodorant.

EPSOM SALTS B.P.
(Magnesium Sulphate B.P.)

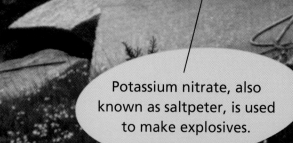

Potassium nitrate, also known as saltpeter, is used to make explosives.

Word Bank   carbohydrate   organic compound that contains carbon, hydrogen, and oxygen

The bacteria in their bodies allow these termites to live on a diet of wood.

Compounds in living things

Carbon compounds in living things are called **organic compounds**. **Proteins** are organic compounds that make up many body tissues in animals. Proteins are long chains of smaller organic compounds. For our bodies to make proteins, we must eat and digest proteins from foods. Meat, fish, beans, and dairy products are good sources of protein.

Carbohydrates are organic compounds of carbon, hydrogen, and oxygen. Starch and sugar are carbohydrates. Fruits, vegetables, and pasta are good sources of the carbohydrates our bodies need for **energy**.

Cooking oils, meat fat, and butter are examples of **lipids**. We need these compounds of carbon, hydrogen, and oxygen to keep our cells working properly. But eating too much of foods that contain lipids can be harmful.

Cellulose is a kind of carbohydrate found in the walls of plant **cells**. Humans cannot digest cellulose. However, certain animals, such as cattle and termites, have special **bacteria** in their stomachs. These bacteria can break down plant cellulose into sugar.

lipid   organic compound that includes fats or oils
organic compound   compound that contains carbon

Mixtures

Fabric mixtures

Many fabrics are mixtures. One shirt label may say the fabric is 80 percent cotton and 20 percent polyester. Another shirt may be 60 percent cotton and 40 percent polyester. The **physical properties** of the shirt fabric are a combination of cotton and polyester properties.

Most things around us are **mixtures.** Soil, ocean water, and even pizza topping are mixtures. Substances in a mixture are not held together by **chemical bonds** like the substances in a **compound.** No new substances form in a mixture. Substances in a mixture also keep their own properties.

Two types of mixture

There are two types of mixture. Ocean water is an example of one type. You cannot see the different parts in this mixture because the materials are so evenly spread out. The other type of mixture has larger parts that are different from each other. Fruit salad is an example. So are rocks. You can see the different parts in the mixture.

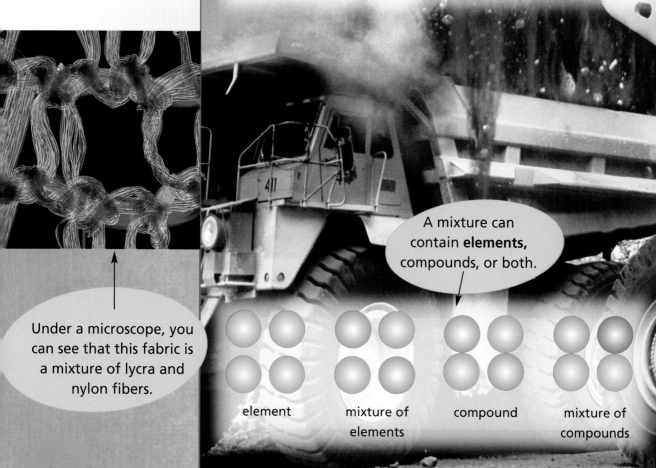

Under a microscope, you can see that this fabric is a mixture of lycra and nylon fibers.

A mixture can contain **elements,** compounds, or both.

element | mixture of elements | compound | mixture of compounds

Word Bank   filter   strain by pouring through paper or cloth

Separating mixtures

It is usually easier to separate a mixture when you can see the different parts. If you do not like grapes, you can just pick them out of a fruit salad. Separating a mixture of solids of different sizes might be as easy as pouring them through a sifter with smaller and smaller holes. A mixture of rocks, pebbles, and sand could be separated in this way.

Filtering can separate a mixture of sand and water. The mixture is poured into a funnel lined with filter paper. The water will pass through the paper but the sand will not. It will be trapped in the filter.

Toothpaste is a mixture.

The substances that make up toothpaste are evenly spread throughout the mixture. But as with any mixture, the substances and their amounts can vary. That is why different toothpastes have different colors or flavors.

The material that is mined at this gravel pit is a mixture of sand, gravel, and other materials.

Solutions

Ocean water

About 3.5 percent of the contents of a glass of ocean water is made up of dissolved solids. Sodium and chloride **ions** from dissolved salt make up almost 86 percent of this **mass.** The graph below shows the other solids that are dissolved in ocean water.

If you mix sugar and water together, the two **compounds** do not change. But the sugar seems to disappear. The pieces of sugar separate into sugar **molecules,** so they are too small to be seen. We say the sugar **dissolves** in the water. This **mixture** is called a **solution.** In a solution one substance is spread evenly throughout the other substance. In a solution of sugar and water, the sugar molecules are spread evenly through the water. The substance that dissolves in a solution is called the **solute.** The substance it dissolves in is the **solvent.** When sugar dissolves in water, sugar is the solute and water is the solvent.

Ocean Water

- water (96.5%)
- dissolved solids (3.5%)

Dissolved solids in ocean water

- chloride (55.0%)
- sodium (30.6%)
- sulfate (7.7%)
- magnesium (3.7%)
- calcium (1.2%)
- potassium (1.1%)
- other (0.7%)

This shark is swimming in a solution. Ocean water has many substances dissolved in it.

concentrated   containing a large amount of solute
dilute   containing a small amount of solute

Foods like ham are preserved with salt or sugar. This removes water from the meat. Drier foods last much longer than fresh foods.

Describing solutions

Solutions can be either weak or strong. A weak solution has a small amount of dissolved solute. Such a solution is called **dilute.** A strong solution has a large amount of dissolved solute. Such a solution is said to be **concentrated.** If a colored solute is dissolved in water, the darker the color of the solution and the more concentrated it is.

As you add more and more sugar to a glass of water, the solution becomes more concentrated. Finally, no more sugar will dissolve in the water. The solution is **saturated** and cannot dissolve any more solute. Any extra sugar added will settle at the bottom of the glass.

Preserving foods

Water can pass into and out of the **cells** of living things. This causes the cells to swell or shrink. Water passes from a dilute solution to a more concentrated solution through a cell wall. The cells of foods placed in a concentrated salt or sugar solution will lose water.

saturated containing as much solute as can be dissolved at that temperature

Dissolving solids in liquids

The most common kind of **solution** is a solid **dissolved** in a liquid. Salt or sugar dissolved in water forms this kind of solution.

How fast a **solute** dissolves in a **solvent** depends on the size of the solute **particles.** The smaller the particles are, the faster they mix with the solvent. If sugar and water are mixed, small grains of sugar will dissolve faster than the same amount of sugar in a cube. Stirring will also make the sugar dissolve faster.

Temperature affects how much solute will dissolve. More solid will usually dissolve in a liquid if the temperature is raised. Hot water will dissolve more sugar than cold water.

Adding salt to water will lower the temperature at which water freezes. That is why salt is added to ice cream.

Many cooks add salt to the water in which they cook pasta. The salt raises the temperature at which the water boils. The more salt that is added, the higher the boiling point will be. If the water is hotter, the pasta will cook a little faster.

Word Bank   dissolve   to break down into molecules and mix evenly and completely
solute   substance that dissolves in another substance

Dissolving gases in liquids

Gases, such as ammonia, oxygen, and carbon dioxide, also dissolve in water. Ammonia dissolved in water is used for cleaning. Oxygen, nitrogen, and carbon dioxide from the air dissolve in the water of lakes, oceans, and rivers. Without the dissolved oxygen in the water, fish would not be able to live.

Unlike a solid, less gas will dissolve in a liquid if the temperature is raised. Carbonated drinks are solutions in which carbon dioxide is dissolved. A glass of soft drink gets "flat" if it sits in a warm room because the carbon dioxide gas comes out of the solution. Stirring also makes a gas come out of a solution. Bubbles of carbon dioxide gas will come out of a soft drink if you stir it.

When an aquarium is first filled, it needs to sit for a while before fish are added. Chlorine gas is used to purify tap water. This gas must be allowed to escape or it could kill the fish.

Fast Fact

The **mixture** of gases found in air forms a solution. Oxygen, carbon dioxide, and other gases are dissolved in nitrogen gas.

Hot fish

Fish depend on oxygen dissolved in the water. As water passes over their gills, oxygen is taken into their blood. People who have aquariums must keep an eye on the water temperature. If the water becomes too warm, there will not be enough oxygen dissolved in it. Then the fish can die of suffocation.

Mineral deposits have formed around the edges of this hot spring. The hot water rising from the spring is **saturated** with minerals. The water cools at the earth's surface. Then the minerals come out of solution. This is because less of the minerals can be dissolved at a lower temperature.

Orange and lemon oils are used as flavorings in foods.

Lemons and oranges have oils in their peels. The fruits are rolled over sharp points that pierce tiny pouches in the skin that contain oil. Then the fruit is pressed to squeeze out the juice and oil. The oil rises to the top of the juice, where it can be collected.

Dissolving liquids in liquids

Water is a liquid that can **dissolve** many different substances. Other liquids, such as alcohol, will dissolve in water. People who live in cold places put antifreeze in their car radiators. This **solution** of water and alcohol helps keep the water in the radiator from freezing in cold weather. Vinegar is a solution of two liquids—water and ethanoic acid.

Water cannot be used to put out some fires. These include burning liquids such as oil or gasoline. These liquids do not dissolve in water. Spraying water on them would only spread the fire. For these kinds of fires, a fire extinguisher marked "Class B" should be used.

chromatography   method used to separate colors in a mixture of inks or dyes

Not all liquids will dissolve in water to form solutions. Oil will not dissolve in water. If you mix oil and water and stir, they will separate and the oil will float on top of the water. Oil and water can be separated using a **separating funnel** in the laboratory.

Separating solutions

Filtering cannot take apart substances in a solution. But there are ways of separating solutions. You can separate a solid dissolved in a liquid by letting it sit until the liquid **evaporates.** When the liquid evaporates, the solid will be left behind.

You can separate a gas dissolved in a liquid by heating the liquid. The gas will escape into the air, leaving the liquid behind.

Solutions of liquids can be separated by **fractional distillation.** The **mixture** is heated and each liquid changes to a gas at a different temperature. As each liquid boils off, the gas is collected. Air can be cooled until it changes to a liquid. Then as it warms, the gases in the air can be separated.

Fast Facts

- Crude oil is a mixture that is separated into its different parts by fractional distillation. These parts include gasoline, paraffin, and diesel fuel.
- When oil is spilled in the ocean, it is very hard to separate it from the water. Floating oil is a **pollutant** that washes up on beaches. It harms all kinds of living things.

Chromatography

Chromatography can be used to separate a mixture of colored substances. A small drop of the mixture is placed near the bottom of a piece of filter paper and allowed to dry. The paper is placed in a container so the bottom edge just touches the **solvent.** As the solvent travels up the paper, the colored substances separate.

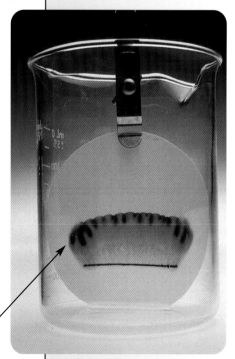

This picture shows the different colors in the black ink of a marker pen. The ink used here dissolved in water, so water was the solvent.

More Mixtures

If you fill a jar with pond water, you might notice that the water looks slightly muddy. If you let the **mixture** stand, soil **particles** settle to the bottom of the jar. The solid particles that settle to the bottom are called **sediment.**

Particles in suspensions

A mixture of soil and water is an example of a **suspension.** A suspension is a cloudy mixture of two or more materials that separate if left standing. Suspensions look well mixed at first, but in time they always separate. You can separate

The parts of blood in this tube were separated by a machine called a **centrifuge.** A centrifuge spins the tube at high speeds and the suspended particles are pulled to the bottom of the tube.

Blood

Blood is a mixture that is both a **solution** and a suspension. Blood contains **dissolved** solids and gases. But it also contains suspended solids. The clear yellowish part of blood contains the dissolved solids and gases. The suspended solids include red and white blood cells.

As a river flows, it wears away bits of soil and rock from the land. These materials are carried by the water in suspension.

decant   to pour off liquid gently without disturbing the sediment

a sediment from the liquid above it by **decanting,** or carefully pouring off the liquid. Decanting can be used in the laboratory. It is also used at home when pouring the syrup from a can of fruit pieces or pouring away the oil or water from a can of tuna fish.

Separating suspensions

Particles in a suspension settle on standing. Large particles settle out quickly. Smaller particles take longer to settle. Sand and clay form a suspension in water. The sand will settle to the bottom in a few minutes. But the tiny clay particles will take hours to settle to the bottom.

One way to separate a suspension quickly is by **filtering.** A suspension is poured through a filter made of paper or other material. Filters have tiny holes through which some things can pass but others cannot. Particles that are larger than the holes in the filter cannot pass through. Most drinking water is filtered before it reaches our homes.

River deltas

When a large river empties into an ocean, it slows down. The materials carried in suspension settle to the bottom. Some rivers, such as the Mississippi and the Nile, drop so much suspended material that the ocean cannot wash it away.

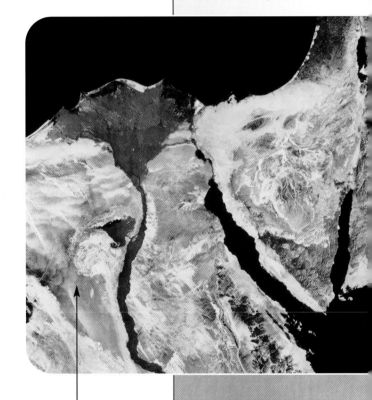

Piles of sediment build up and form new land called a delta. The fan-shaped delta reaches into the ocean.

sediment   undissolved solids that fall to the bottom of a liquid
suspension   mixture containing a liquid in which particles settle

Colloids

Whipped cream, fog, clouds, and smoke are all **colloids**. A colloid is a **mixture** in which the **particles** do not separate on standing. The particles in a colloid are not as small as particles in a **solution.** But they are much smaller than the particles in a **suspension.** Because the particles in a colloid are so small, they cannot be separated by filtration. Particles in a colloid stay mixed because they are always bumping into particles around them.

Whipped cream is a colloid of a gas (air) in a liquid (cream). Fog and clouds are colloids of a liquid (water vapor) in a gas (air). And smoke is a colloid of a solid (dust and other solids) in a gas (air). **Gels,** such as gelatin desserts and jellies, are colloids of solids in a liquid.

Sewage treatment plants use a colloid to trap bacteria.

colloid   mixture with a particle size between that of solutions and suspensions

Emulsions

An **emulsion** is a colloid made of droplets of liquid in another liquid. A material called an **emulsifying agent** is needed to keep the colloid from separating. Many detergents contain emulsifying agents. These break grease into smaller particles, which form an emulsion with water. The grease is then washed away in the water. Egg yolk is the emulsifying agent that keeps the oil and vinegar in mayonnaise from separating.

Colloids, including emulsions, have an unusual property. That property is the ability to scatter light. If a beam of light is passed through a colloid, the beam can be seen from all directions. Car headlight beams can be seen in fog because water droplets in the air scatter the light.

Mixing milk

The cream in fresh milk separates and rises to the top of the milk mixture. To stop this dairies use a process called **homogenization**. This breaks the cream into very small colloidal particles. When these particles are mixed with the rest of the milk, they stay mixed, forming an emulsion.

Tiny particles of dust and water in the air make the lighthouse beam visible.

Alloys

Mouth metals

Dentists sometimes use an alloy called **amalgam** to fill cavities in teeth. An amalgam is an alloy that contains mercury. Dental amalgam is a mixture of mercury, silver, and zinc. It is a liquid when first made, but it quickly hardens.

An **alloy** is a **mixture** of a **metal** and one or more other **elements.** Aluminum alloys are used to make products ranging from foil food wraps to airplane bodies. Designers of aircraft and aerospace systems like to use aluminum alloys because they are lightweight and strong.

Bronze is an alloy of copper and tin. Bronze is used in plumbing fixtures and in hardware that will come into contact with saltwater, because the tin does not react with chemicals in seawater. Brass is an alloy of copper and zinc. Brass is used in musical instruments and in some hardware. Sterling silver is an alloy of silver and copper used in tableware. Solder is an alloy of lead and tin used by plumbers to connect metal pipes.

An alloy is used by dentists to repair cavities in teeth.

alloy   mixture of a metal and one or more other elements
amalgam   alloy that contains mercury

Steel

The many different kinds of steel make up an important group of alloys. All types of steel are alloys of iron and carbon. But many also have other metals mixed in. Different steel alloys are made for different uses. Manganese steel is very hard. It is used in railway tracks and armor plating on military tanks. Stainless steel is used in surgical tools because it is strong and does not **corrode**. High-speed steel is a steel alloy that contains chromium and tungsten. It is used in cutting tools, drill bits, and saw blades because it keeps its sharp, hard edge even when it heats up during cutting.

Mending bodies

Newer alloys are lighter and stronger than steel. This makes them perfect for using inside the body, as this X-ray shows.

Some of the first materials put into human bodies were alloys of steel. Stainless steel is made of iron, chromium, and nickel. It was used to make plates and screws for joining broken bones. More recently, alloys containing titanium or cobalt have been used instead.

Pure gold is soft and bends easily. Copper is harder than gold. So alloys of gold and copper are used to make jewelry. The copper adds strength to the gold.

corrode   to damage by a reaction with chemicals

Further Information

Organizations

Science Made Simple

Learn about science "hands on." Site includes science news, projects, facts, more. sciencemadesimple.com

Rader Studios

Fun science news, plus activities including quizzes, experiments, tutorials, and more. chem4kids.com

Lawrence Livermore National Laboratory

Get the latest science news from a national security laboratory. llnl.gov

Books

Oxlade, Chris. *Chemicals in Action: Elements and Compounds.* Chicago: Heinemann Library, 2002.

Oxlade, Chris. *Science Answers: Changing Materials.* Chicago: Heinemann InfoSearch, 2003.

Snedden, Robert. *Materials World: Materials Technology.* Chicago: Heinemann Library, 2001.

Snedden, Robert. *Materials World: Separating Materials.* Chicago: Heinemann Library, 2001.

World Wide Web

If you want to find out more about **compounds, mixtures,** and **solutions,** you can search the Internet using keywords like these:

- emulsions
- chemical formulas
- compounds + properties
- compounds + mixtures + solutions
- colloids + examples
- [name of a metal] + ore + mining
- mixtures + separating

You can also find your own keywords by using headings or words from this book. Use the search tips opposite to help you find the most useful websites.

Search tips

There are billions of pages on the Internet so it can be difficult to find exactly what you are looking for. For example, if you just type in "water" on a search engine like Google, you'll get a list of 85 million web pages. These search skills will help you find useful websites more quickly:

- Know exactly what you want to find out about first.
- Use simple keywords instead of whole sentences.
- Use two to six keywords in a search, putting the most important words first.
- Be precise—only use names of people, places, or things.
- If you want to find words that go together, put quote marks around them, for example "covalent bond."
- Use the advanced section of your search engine.
- Use the + sign to add certain words to your search.

Where to search

Search engines

A search engine looks through the entire web and lists all the sites that match the words in the search box. It can give thousands of links, but the best matches are at the top of the list, on the first page. Try **google.com**

Search directory

A search directory is more like a library of websites that have been sorted by a person instead of a computer. You can search by keyword or subject and browse through the different sites in the same way you would look through books on a library shelf. A good example is **yahooligans.com**

Glossary

acid compound that contains hydrogen and has a pH of less than 7

alkali base that will dissolve in water

alloy mixture of a metal and one or more other elements

amalgam alloy that contains mercury

atom smallest particle of an element

bacteria tiny living things so small they can only be seen with a microscope

base compound that feels slippery and has pH of more than 7

brittle firm, but easily broken

carbohydrate organic compound that contains carbon, hydrogen, and oxygen

cells building blocks that make up all living things

centrifuge machine that spins suspensions at high speeds to make suspended particles settle out quickly

chemical bond strong attraction between two atoms

chemical property feature of a substance that tells us how it will react

chemical reaction change that produces one or more new substances

chemical symbol short way of writing the name of an element

chromatography method used to separate colors in a mixture of inks or dyes

colloid mixture with a particle size between that of solutions and suspensions

compound substance made of atoms of more than one element

compound ion group of atoms that has an electric charge and acts together in a chemical reaction

concentrated containing a large amount of solute

corrode damage by a chemical reaction

covalent compound compound formed when atoms join and share electrons

crystal solid in which particles are arranged in an orderly, repeating pattern

decant to pour off liquid gently without disturbing the sediment

dilute containing a small amount of solute

dissolve to break down into molecules and mix evenly and completely

electrical charge amount of electricity on something

electron tiny, negatively charged particle outside the nucleus of an atom

element substance made of only one kind of atom

emulsifying agent material that keeps liquids in a colloid from separating

emulsion colloid made of droplets of liquid in another liquid

energy ability to cause change

evaporate change from a liquid to a gas

filter strain by pouring through paper or cloth

formula symbols and numbers used to show how elements are joined

fractional distillation separating a mixture of liquids by heating

gel colloid of solids in a liquid

hazardous dangerous or harmful

homogenization process that breaks cream into tiny particles so that they do not separate from the milk

ion atom or group of atoms with an electric charge

ionic compound compound formed when a nonmetal takes electrons from a metal

lipid organic compound that includes fats or oils

mass amount of matter in an object. It is measured in grams or kilograms

matter anything that takes up space and has mass

metal element with certain properties

mineral nonliving solid material

mixture material made of elements or compounds not joined chemically

molecule two or more atoms held together by chemical bonds

neutron particle with no charge, found in the nucleus of an atom

nonmetal element without metallic properties

nucleus center of an atom, made of protons and neutrons

ore metal that is found combined with other elements

organic compound compound that contains carbon

particle tiny piece

physical change change in how something looks, not in what makes it up

physical property feature that can be seen or measured without changing what the substance is made of

pollutant harmful substance in the air, in water, or on land

protein organic compound that contains nitrogen and is made of long chains of smaller organic compounds

proton positively charged particle in the nucleus of an atom

pure substance matter that is the same throughout

reduction process of removing oxygen from an ore

salt compound formed when an acid reacts with a base; sodium chloride is a common salt

saturated containing as much solute as can be dissolved at that temperature

sediment undissolved solids that fall to the bottom of a liquid

separating funnel laboratory tool used to separate two liquids that do not dissolve in each other

solute substance that dissolves in another substance

solution mixture in which one substance dissolves in another

solvent substance that dissolves a solute

state of matter whether something is solid, liquid, or gas

suspension mixture containing a liquid in which particles settle after a time

ultraviolet (UV) light invisible light energy from the sun

water cycle cycle of water from liquid to ice to gas on the earth

Index